The Archers

Compiled by
Liz Rigbey

D0714314

BBC BOOKS

BBC QUIZBOOKS

Telly Addicts
Masterteam
Brain of Sport
First Class
Trivia Test Match
Superscot
Telly Addicts 2
Food & Drink
The Archers
Beat the Teacher

Published by BBC Books,
a division of BBC Enterprises Limited,
Woodlands, 80 Wood Lane, London W12 0TT
First published 1988

© British Broadcasting Corporation 1988
Foreword © Liz Rigbey 1988

ISBN 0 563 20709 4

Set in 10/11pt Plantin by Wilmaset, Wirral
Printed and bound in Great Britain by Richard Clay, Suffolk
Cover printed by Fletchers, Norwich

CONTENTS

FOREWORD

The Archers' listeners are a clever bunch. Forget any ideas you may have of whole families grouped round the crystal set, passively awaiting the next thrilling instalment of Ambridge farm life. No, listeners like to play an active part in their programme, and that means proving the editor wrong whenever possible.

'Have another piece of walnut slice, dear,' says Jill to Phil Archer innocently one teatime, and millions of listeners rise, roaring from their chairs.

'Don't you know he doesn't *like* walnut slice, woman!' they yell angrily at the radio. 'Don't you remember he told you so in *1959*'!

Letters are penned, angry ones. They are sent to me and copied to the Director General to show me how serious the writer is. The gist is always the same: how can we believe in these people if you destroy our illusions with continuity errors?

The fact is that in thirty-seven years of broadcasting, countless continuity errors have been made. The complex set of cards we keep on each character and story-line prove this. Editors spend a great deal of their time trying to mask these mistakes (their own and their predecessors') and attempting to rewrite history without anyone noticing. Sadly, the listening public can rarely be fooled.

Here then, is my own contribution to the endless battle over Archers mythology which is fought between listeners and production team. I hope you enjoy it.

Liz Rigbey
Editor
The Archers

FAMILY TREES

1   Who is Doris Archer's brother?

2   How many children do Pat and Tony have?

3   Laura Archer came to Ambridge from New Zealand in the late 1950s. Her husband was dead. Who was he?

4   Who was Mrs Perkins' son-in-law?

5   Name Eddie Grundy's jailbird brother.

6   Who are Jethro and Lizzie Larkin's two daughters?

7   Whom did Valerie Trentham marry after the death of her husband Reggie?

8   Walter Gabriel discovered he had a granddaughter in 1986. Who are her natural parents?

9   Who was Jennifer Aldridge's first husband?

10 What was the relationship between Ned and Jethro Larkin?

11 Who is the sister of Jennifer Aldridge and Tony Archer?

12 Who became Grace Fairbrother's stepmother?

FAMILY TREES

1   Tom Forrest.

2   Three: John, Helen and Thomas.

3   Dan's brother Frank.

4   The alcoholic Jack Archer, husband of Peggy.

5   Alf.

6   Rosie Mabbott, married and living in Great Yarmouth, and Clarrie Grundy, now matriarch of Grange Farm.

7   Jack Woolley.

8   Nelson Gabriel and Nancy Tarrant. Nancy had the child, Rosemary, adopted.

9   Roger Travers-Macy, now also remarried.

10   Jethro was Ned's son.

11   Lilian Bellamy.

12   Mrs Helen Carey.

EASY QUESTIONS

1   Which city is closest to Ambridge?

2   Which market town is closest to Ambridge?

3   If you call at the village shop in Ambridge, who is most likely to serve you?

4   Who is the youngest child in Ambridge with the surname Archer?

5   What is the occupation of Christine Barford, née Archer?

6   Which couple moved into Ambridge Hall in 1986?

7   Shula Hebden has ARICS after her name. What is her job?

8   What is the Grundys' favourite watering hole (apart from The Bull)?

9   Who is the oldest inhabitant of the village?

10   What is the name of Kathy Perks' stepdaughter?

11   What are most farmers in Ambridge busy doing in June?

12   Jack Woolley has a swimming pool. Who else in Ambridge has one?

EASY QUESTIONS

1   Felpersham.

2   Borchester.

3   Martha Woodford.

4   Tommy Archer, son of Tony and Pat.

5   She owns and runs a riding stables.

6   The Snells.

7   Land agent. She is an Associate of the Royal
    Institution of Chartered Surveyors.

8   The Cat and Fiddle.

9   Walter Gabriel.

10 Lucy.

11 Haymaking.

12 The Aldridges.

Q | 1950s

1 When did Dan stop using horses and start using tractors?

2 Who offered to replace Jane Maxwell as farm worker, under the close supervision of Phil Archer?

3 Nelson Gabriel did National Service in which of the armed forces?

4 Jack and Peggy Archer moved away from the village to start another smallholding. Where did they go?

5 What was Christine's job in the early 1950s, before she started working with horses?

6 When the mysterious John Tregorran arrived in Ambridge, what was eventually revealed as his previous employment?

7 Which terrible disease hit the stock at Brookfield, taking Dan out of dairying for some time?

8 Walter gave Mrs P a present in the hope that she'd marry him. What was it?

9 Landowner Charles Grenville had a mysterious French housekeeper. What was her name?

10 Grenville arrived in Ambridge because he was an old friend of which local family?

11 Who was farm manager to George Fairbrother?

12 In 1952, who was paid compensation when an aircraft crashed in one of his fields?

1 1951, almost as soon as *The Archers* was first heard. He was slightly behind most farmers in making the change.

2 Grace Fairbrother.

3 The RAF.

4 Cornwall.

5 She worked at Borchester Dairies as a milk sampler.

6 University lecturer.

7 Foot and mouth. All cloven-hooved livestock had to be shot and buried.

8 A pony and trap. Instead she took Arthur Perkins for a ride in it one day, he proposed, and the rest is history.

9 Madame Garonne.

10 The Lawson-Hopes.

11 Phil Archer.

12 Dan Archer.

1 Who was knocked unconscious by an intruder escaping from her home?

2 Whose relation was Hugo Barnaby?

3 Jill was informed by a village schoolteacher that one of her children was backward. Which one?

4 Roger Patillo arrived in the village but this was discovered to be a pseudonym. What was the stranger's real name?

5 Who represented the Ambridge WI at a Buckingham Palace Garden Party?

6 Who was wrongly accused of being the father of Jennifer's illegitimate baby?

7 For what profession did Jennifer train?

8 Albert Bates replaced Geoffrey Bryden in what important job in Ambridge?

9 Love-letters written by a former boyfriend were stolen from which newly-wed?

10 Why did Elizabeth Archer require an operation soon after she was born?

11 Whose friends persuaded him to go to the optician because they feared he was unfit to drive?

12 Where did Phil and Jill live for eight years prior to their move to Brookfield?

1960s

1 Doris. The listening public was to learn from this what the Criminal Injuries Compensation Board was, and how to claim damages in such an event.

2 He was an American cousin of John Tregorran's.

3 Shula. How wrong that teacher was!

4 Roger Travers-Macy.

5 Doris.

6 Nelson Gabriel.

7 Teaching.

8 Village bobby.

9 Carol Grenville. The former boyfriend was her future husband, John Tregorran.

10 She was born with a heart condition.

11 Walter Gabriel's, and Jack Archer in particular.

12 Hollowtree, previously called Allard's Farm.

Q 1970s

1   Who lodged with Martha and Joby Woodford before moving to Nightingale Farm?

2   Lucy Perks was rushed to hospital when she was still a toddler. Why?

3   Shula set off in 1979 to visit her friend Michele Brown in New Zealand. How had she met Michele?

4   Who allowed a Mr Nolan from Liverpool to carry out some tarmacking: and found him untraceable when the weeds showed through?

5   Which couple celebrated their golden wedding anniversary in 1971?

6   Ralph and Lilian Bellamy had a son in 1973. What is his name?

7   Who came second in the best publican competition?

8   Who announced to Jill Archer in 1977 that he would welcome Shula as a daughter-in-law?

9   Who shocked her husband by setting off for a holiday in Paris with her friend Sheila?

10 Who was left £4200 by his Uncle Charlie?

11 On which day of the year was Pat and Tony's first son, John Daniel, born?

12 Why did Walter Gabriel move in with Dan and Doris in 1977 (where he outstayed his welcome)?

A 1970s

1 Neil Carter.

2 She had taken some of her grandmother's sleeping pills.

3 Michele had come to Ambridge in a sheep-shearing gang. The friends' reunion in New Zealand never took place.

4 Haydn Evans. Nolan tarmacked his garage forecourt for just £120. No wonder the price was so low.

5 Dan and Doris Archer.

6 James.

7 Polly Perks.

8 Joe Grundy.

9 Jill Archer.

10 Jethro Larkin.

11 He was born on 31 December as the New Year (1976) was being rung in.

12 The roof had blown off his cottage.

Q 1980s

1   Who sold swimming pools, although not many?

2   Who collided with the Tuckers' milk-float?

3   Who tried to sneak into bed with Shula and found himself in bed with Phil instead?

4   Who was fooled into thinking he had heard the first cuckoo and wrote to the *Borchester Echo* about it, against all advice?

5   Why is Dick Pearson important in the life of Eddie Grundy?

6   Who gave whom a pair of purple legwarmers for her birthday in 1986?

7   Who gave her chair to a burglar?

8   Which newcomer staggered the locals by turning up at the Cricket Club dinner in an MCC tie?

9   Why did Grey Gables have to be closed for Christmas 1986?

10 What resolution at the Ambridge WI affected takings at the village shop?

11 Who threatened to bring a private prosecution against George Barford when George 'helped him over the stile'?

12 Jill was giving Laura Archer a driving lesson when the car struck something which Joe Grundy was only too pleased to remove. What was it?

1980s

1   Nigel Pargetter.

2   Nigel Pargetter.

3   Nigel Pargetter.

4   Not Nigel Pargetter, but Colonel Danby, who was deceived by Eddie Grundy's cuckoo imitation.

5   He is landlord of The Cat and Fiddle.

6   Walter gave them to Mrs Perkins: she is not on record as having worn them.

7   Mrs Perkins. She thought he was going to upholster it at a special OAP rate, but it was never seen again.

8   Robert Snell.

9   It was infested with rats, causing an outbreak of salmonella.

10 The WI members agreed to stop using aerosols containing CFCs, which damage the earth's ozone layer.

11 Ben Warner.

12 A deer. There was venison for dinner at Grange Farm for weeks.

FARMING (1)

1 Name the two farmers in Ambridge who keep sheep.

2 What colour are Phil Archer's cows?

3 Which Ambridge farmer diversified into deer farming?

4 It was wrongly rumoured in Ambridge that Phil Archer was testing BST on his dairy herd on behalf of a drug company. What is BST?

5 How did Lucy Perks contaminate Phil's milk?

6 Which agricultural college did Ruth Pritchard leave Brookfield to attend?

7 Who is so brilliant that she was able to learn everything about farming from a one-week course?

8 Whose organic crops were sprayed in error by Brian Aldridge's man?

9 What is the name of the production allocation imposed on every dairy farmer in 1984?

10 In winter farmers in Ambridge now feed their stock on a fodder which was almost unknown when Dan Archer was young. What is it?

11 Joe Grundy talks acres but the Ministry of Agriculture talks hectares. Which are larger?

12 Whose dairy herd was discovered to have TB in 1982?

A FARMING (1)

1. Brian Aldridge and Phil Archer. The Bellamy Estate also has sheep.

2. Black and white – they're Friesians, like 90 per cent of cows in Britain. Since the 1960s, these cows have dominated British dairying.

3. Brian Aldridge.

4. It is a hormone used to increase a cow's milk yield.

5. By pushing the tank washer button while milk was still in the tank. This is easy to do. Lucy learned the trick when Ruth did it by mistake.

6. Harper Adams in Shropshire.

7. Lynda Snell.

8. Carol Tregorran's. The incident happened at a time when relations were already strained, due to John's interest in Jennifer Aldridge.

9. The milk quota.

10. Silage. This has replaced hay as the main winter fodder crop. Hay is dried grass; silagemaking conserves the grass by pickling it in its own acid.

11. Hectares; there are about 2.5 acres in a hectare.

12. Mike Tucker's.

Q GENERAL QUESTIONS (1)

1 Who did Mrs Perkins live with when she first arrived in Ambridge?

2 Who was Red Knight and what was his sad fate?

3 Matthew Thorogood isn't the first doctor to have a branch surgery in Ambridge. Who was doctor to Jack Archer throughout his long illness?

4 Did humble scribe Simon Parker ever become editor of the *Borchester Echo*?

5 Who is the only known owner of a gorilla suit in Borsetshire?

6 What is Mrs Perkins' first name?

7 What careers advice was Shula given prior to A levels? It was advice of which Phil very much approved.

8 Kathy Perks stayed a night at The Bull long before she married Sid. She didn't want to go home in case she met someone. Who?

9 Which Ambridge child shocked her mother by entering a painting for a competition, part of which she had traced?

10 Who brought so much furniture when she first moved to Ambridge that it had to be stored in Walter Gabriel's barn?

11 Lucy Perks was caught contaminating milk at Brookfield Farm. What was her motive?

12 Who officiated at the marriage of Joby Woodford and Martha Lily on Christmas Day 1972?

A GENERAL QUESTIONS (1)

1 Bill Oakley. He died shortly afterwards . . .

2 A horse, regularly ridden by the horse-mad teenage Shula. He was struck by a car and had to be destroyed.

3 Dr McLaren.

4 Yes indeed. As editor, he admirably refused to tailor his news stories to the interests of his overbearing proprietor, Jack Woolley.

5 Nigel Pargetter. He was unleashed upon a listening public in 1983 wearing only his gorilla suit.

6 Her husbands called her Polly: her real name is Mary.

7 It was suggested that Shula became a vet, but it was rapidly revealed that her interest in animals was limited to horses.

8 Her husband. The couple were separated but he was anxious to revive their relationship.

9 Lucy Perks. Doris bought the painting in a charity auction but, when Polly confessed, Doris insisted on keeping it.

10 Mrs Perkins.

11 She believed Brookfield was one of the farms being used by drug companies to test the hormone, Bovine Somatotrophin (BST), and was worried about its effect on both the animal and the consumer.

12 A retired parson, as the vicar was ill. He was called Canon Meridew.

PRITE ENTERPRISE
PRIVATE ENTERPRISE (1)

1 Dorothy Adamson worked in which Borchester boutique – until its owner lost so much money that he went into antiques instead?

2 Tom and Pru opened what new venture to the public for Jack Woolley in the 1970s? Of course, it was nothing but a worry to them.

3 Who went fish farming – for a while?

4 Who planned to build a motel extension to The Bull? The idea was abandoned when it was proved to be uneconomic.

5 Who grows grapes and makes Ambridge wine?

6 Betty Tucker once made and sold what kind of cheese?

7 Who set up a farm shop with Carol Tregorran in the 1970s?

8 Harry Booker, sometime postman and entrepreneur, tried to start a Sunday market in Ambridge on the Pounds' farm. What was his connection with the Pounds?

9 Jennifer Aldridge and John Tregorran, amid rumours that they were having an affair, co-wrote a book. What was it about?

10 Which couple tried breeding sheepdogs but gave it up when they made no money?

11 Which villager tried, with many mishaps, to run his own bus service for Ambridge?

12 Walter Gabriel, Bill Sawyer and Agatha Turvey went into what sort of business together in 1961?

A PRIVATE ENTERPRISE (1)

1 Gear Change. The proprietor was called Otto.

2 A garden centre.

3 Paul Johnson, husband of Christine. The fish farm was later taken over by Jack Woolley and run by Tom.

4 This sounds like one of Jack Archer's mad schemes, but actually it was Sid Perks' idea.

5 The Tregorrans, a project started in 1976.

6 Goats' cheese.

7 The Pounds, at Ambridge Farm.

8 Son-in-law. His wife, Marilyn, was Mary Pound's daughter.

9 The history of Ambridge. It was called *Ambridge, an English Village Through the Ages*.

10 Mike and Betty Tucker.

11 Walter Gabriel.

12 They ran a pet shop. Walter was soon bought out when he failed to pull his weight.

HOBBIES AND SPORTS

1   Who is the greatest country 'n' western singer in Borsetshire and possibly the world?

2   Which villager shared Phil's enthusiasm for cine-photography and took over the running of the local cine-society from him?

3   Who is captain of the village cricket team?

4   a   Who is the team's scorer?
    b   Who makes the tea?

5   What team is Shula still a member of, although she seldom goes to practice?

6   Name Christine's racehorse.

7   Which flower does Jack Woolley enter for flower shows?

8   Jill Archer and Kathy Perks took part in which oratorio?

9   What does Tom Forrest collect?

10   At which game does Neil Carter shine?

11   Which villager was once a successful novelist?

12   Why did Shula Archer's membership of the hunt once cause a scandal in the local paper?

HOBBIES AND SPORTS

1 Eddie Grundy.

2 John Tregorran.

3 David Archer.

4 a Mrs Antrobus.
  b Martha Woodford, when the urn isn't leaking.

5 The bell-ringing team.

6 Ambridge Flyer.

7 Chrysanthemums. Higgs grows them, Jack collects the trophies.

8 *The Messiah*.

9 Coins.

10 Darts.

11 Jennifer. If you answered Mike Daly, you're too clever by half. Daly was a landowner and thriller writer who appeared briefly in the 1950s.

12 She was drawing dole at the time and the newspaper regarded hunting as too expensive a sport for the unemployed.

AMBRIDGE ROMANCES

1   When Phil managed the Fairbrother Estate, for what reason did he employ Jane Maxwell?

2   Who proposed to Elizabeth Archer just before leaving Ambridge?

3   In whom were Joe Blower, Doughy Hood and Harry Cobb all romantically interested?

4   Maggie Price, a friend of Shula's at Borchester Tech., first dated Neil Carter and then someone even closer to Shula. Who?

5   How did Caroline Bone meet Dr Thorogood?

6   How did John and Carol Tregorran first meet?

7   To whom did Jack Woolley propose in 1974?

8   Who borrowed Jack Woolley's Bentley to visit his lady friend near Hollerton?

9   Who canoodled with David Archer, tried to canoodle with Ben Warner and finally proposed to Mark Hebden?

10 Bill Insley and Joe Grundy were both romantically attached to which Ambridge lady?

11 Martha Woodford and Mrs Antrobus each tried to engage Colonel Danby's affections by getting involved in the sport that means most to him. What is it?

12 Who sent valentine cards to Jill, Elizabeth and Shula Archer?

A AMBRIDGE ROMANCES

1 To look after the poultry. In such romantic conditions, of course they soon fell in love.

2 Nigel Pargetter.

3 Each rivalled Walter for Mrs Perkins' affections.

4 Kenton.

5 He was the locum who was called when she fell off Ivor – a fall which occurred when Ivor was frightened by Eddie's reckless tractor driving.

6 His motorbike collided with her new car.

7 Peggy Archer.

8 Jack's chauffeur and handyman, John Higgs.

9 Jackie Woodstock.

10 Martha Woodford.

11 Cricket, Martha made the tea while Mrs Antrobus scored.

12 Nigel Pargetter.

Q THE GREAT UNHEARD

1   What nationality is the chef at Grey Gables?

2   Higgs looks after Jack's Bentley, and another of Jack's joys besides. What?

3   Who was last heard of blowing out the candles on her birthday cake at a surprise tea party organised by Jill?

4   What is Shane's speciality cuisine at the wine bar?

5   What post does Graham Collard hold at Brookfield?

6   Who came all the way across the world for his grandfather's funeral and then was not heard by the listening public?

7   Who lives in the Channel Islands and has great influence in Ambridge, although she seldom visits?

8   Although their love story held listeners spellbound for many years, which married couple have scarcely been heard this decade?

9   Mr Pullen is famous for holding up the Over-60s on their outings. Why?

10 Which member of the Over-60s uses a walking-frame?

11 Who came straight to Ambridge from Gloucester gaol and was seen picking mushrooms but not heard to utter a word?

12 In 1988 who was responsible for pushing up the temperature of the Grey Gables pool to 95° F?

THE GREAT UNHEARD

1 Jean-Paul is French. This temperamental artiste was unheard until 1988.

2 His prize chrysanthemums.

3 Pru Forrest. This was her most sizeable contribution to broadcasting for some years.

4 He has made a life study of the quiche and its many variations.

5 Cowman.

6 Kenton Archer.

7 Lilian Bellamy, owner of the estate.

8 The Tregorrans.

9 He makes constant visits to the lavatory.

10 Mrs Potter.

11 Alf Grundy.

12 John Higgs. He was often seen bobbing about on a lilo in his wraparound sunglasses.

CHILDREN

1 One family fostered children in the 1960s and another adopted a baby. Who were these families?

2 Who told the vicar about her pregnancy before she told her parents?

3 Why did Susan Carter reject her second baby?

4 What was wrong with Susan's first baby, Emma, when she was born prematurely?

5 Which child went ice-skating, although it was forbidden, and had to be rescued by her father?

6 Name the pony Pat and Tony borrowed and then bought from the Aldridges for Helen.

7 Which child loves American football?

8 Where does William Grundy go to school?

9 Who had her fourth child at the age of forty-three?

10 Tony Archer was prosecuted when his son John was discovered doing what?

11 Which exceptionally musical child grew up to have little interest in playing the piano, except when she is angry?

12 Who is older: David, or the twins, Kenton and Shula?

CHILDREN

1   In 1960 Tom and Pru Forrest fostered Peter Stevens and Johnnie Martin, and in 1965 Chris and Paul Johnson adopted baby Peter.

2   Jennifer Archer, when she was carrying Adam.

3   Christopher was born with a cleft lip.

4   She had jaundice.

5   Lilian Archer.

6   Velvet, Peggy helped buy him.

7   John Archer.

8   Loxley Barratt. Clarrie drives him there herself every day.

9   Jennifer Aldridge.

10   Driving a tractor under the age of thirteen.

11   Elizabeth Archer.

12   The twins.

THE COUNTRYSIDE (1)

1 What did Jack Woolley call the otter which took up brief residence on the Am by Grey Gables?

2 Which owl shrieks and which one hoots 'to-whit-to-woo'?

3 What is a giant puffball and what does Joe Grundy do with it?

4 At Brookfield, David lets wood lie for several years before taking it indoors to burn . . . but which wood can be burnt 'green'?

5 Newcomers to Ambridge assume that the big black birds congregating by the barn conversions are crows. Are they?

6 Lynda Snell discovered a rare tree on the Bellamy Estate: it has grey bark, leaves a bit like a maple's and speckled brown fruit in September. What is it?

7 Joe Grundy's cider is legendary. What is his equally lethal pear-brew called?

8 When is the first cuckoo heard in Ambridge?

9 The bluebells in Leaders Wood are usually out in which month?

10 When Tom talks about tree rats, what does he mean?

11 Brian Aldridge has ploughed up one of his footpaths. Under what circumstances is this not against the law?

12 Tony's barn has birds nesting under its eaves each summer: are they swallows or housemartins?

THE COUNTRYSIDE (1)

1 Tarka. This startlingly original name is still used for the hotel's bar: The Tarka the Otter Bar.

2 The barn owl shrieks eerily and the tawny owl 'to-whit-to-woos'.

3 A balloon-like fungus which can be found in pastures during August. Joe eats his sliced and fried in dripping with a little salt.

4 Ash.

5 No. If they congregate, they're rooks. Crows are more solitary, seen singly or in pairs.

6 A wild service tree. The Nature Conservancy Council later declared the area a Site of Special Scientific Interest, to Lynda's delight.

7 Perry.

8 Mid-April – rarely before the 17th.

9 May.

10 Grey squirrels.

11 Brian must reinstate the path (perhaps by rolling it) within a fortnight.

12 Housemartins. Swallows prefer to nest inside the barn.

CRIME

1 Who stole chocolate Santas from Martha's shop?

2 Who went out to tea with Doris Archer and had her handbag stolen?

3 Who believed her handbag stolen in Torquay, and was embarrassed to find it safe?

4 Who came to Ambridge after spending several years at an approved school for breaking and entering?

5 Polly Perks had a miscarriage caused when she was the victim of a crime. What crime?

6 What disaster befell Adam Macy when he was only three?

7 Whose tenants did a moonlight flit, leaving little furniture and owing a large sum in back rent?

8 Carol Tregorran was accused of which crime in 1975?

9 Who was with Jack Woolley in 1973 when he was attacked by a gang robbing Grey Gables?

10 Shula caught a man she was very fond of carrying out a burglary in Ambridge. Who was he, and whom was he robbing at the time?

11 Tom Forrest was acquitted of the manslaughter of Bob Larkin. What relation was Bob of that sturdy Brookfield worker, Ned Larkin?

12 Which crime shocked all of Ambridge in 1977? It was the first known occurrence in the area.

A CRIME

1   Lucy Perks. Martha told Sid, but incredibly, not the rest of the village.

2   Mrs Perkins. It was later returned by the police.

3   Doris Archer.

4   Sid Perks.

5   She was attacked at the village shop when she was postmistress.

6   He was kidnapped.

7   Sid and Polly Perks' first tenants at Rose Cottage, the Briggs.

8   Shoplifting. She was found not guilty.

9   Hazel Woolley. The crooks succeeded in gagging her, something many villagers have since wished they could do.

10 Ben Warner. He was robbing Peggy's Blossom Hill Cottage, latest in a chain of local robberies.

11 Brother. Bob was the black sheep of the family.

12 The church was robbed, of the Offertory Plate and two candlesticks.

GENERAL QUESTIONS (2)

1 What did Nigel Pargetter and Elizabeth Archer both sell in the summer of 1986?

2 What was the special talent of Peter Stevens, foster child of Pru and Tom Forrest?

3 Which Ambridge baby was born on Christmas Eve?

4 Why didn't John Tregorran need to work when he first came to Ambridge?

5 You can be sure of hearing country'n'western music blaring out if you visit Grange Farm . . . but which other couple are c'n'w enthusiasts?

6 Who found her holiday cancelled when the Aldridges cancelled theirs?

7 Who is the only person cruel enough ever to have kicked Captain?

8 Who was Sir Jack Woolhay?

9 What do Coverdale, Bryden and Barry all have in common?

10 What do Cavendish, McLaren and Poole have in common?

11 Who bought the Over-60s tea in the hope that they would vote him on to the parish council?

12 For many years, Joby Woodford kept a secret from everyone in the village, except his wife Martha. What was it?

A GENERAL QUESTIONS (2)

1 Mr Snowy ice-creams.

2 He had a flair for things mechanical, and went to work for Haydn Evans at the garage. He now runs a garage in Borchester.

3 Deborah Macy.

4 He'd recently won the football pools.

5 Mike and Betty Tucker.

6 Betty Tucker when she was Jennifer's daily. She'd been looking forward to a week off while the Aldridges were away.

7 Hazel Woolley. Brian Aldridge is probably capable of it, too.

8 The owner of Grey Gables, when it was a manor house 300 years ago. Naturally Jack Woolley assumes himself to be a descendant.

9 They are all policemen who have lived in Ambridge.

10 They are all doctors who have worked in Ambridge.

11 Jack Woolley, ever transparent.

12 He couldn't read.

ROUND AND ABOUT AMBRIDGE

1   In which county is Ambridge?

2   Where does Mrs Walker, cleaner to the gentry, live?

3   The Cat and Fiddle is the wildest bar this side of Laramie. Is it situated on the road to Felpersham, Stratford-upon-Avon or Edgeley?

4   Sheep graze there, Phil goes there to think, Caroline rides there, Nelson wouldn't walk to the top, and Mark proposed to Shula there. Where?

5   Whose pasture, bordering the Bellamy woods, was recently designated of special scientific interest?

6   Where is Nigel Pargetter's ancestral home?

7   A lake is one of the features of the Country Park. It shares its name with a large hall which lies outside Ambridge. Can you name it?

8   The Bellamy Estate is named after its present owners, but by what name is it otherwise known?

9   Caroline Bone's uncle, Lord Netherbourne, lives in which village?

10 At which London station would you catch a train for Ambridge, and where would you get off?

11 A ghostly rider is said to ride across a hill near Ambridge. Which hill and who is the rider?

12 If Ambridge residents want to catch a bus, they have a long walk to the main road. Where does the bus stop?

A ROUND AND ABOUT AMBRIDGE

1 Borsetshire.

2 Penny Hassett.

3 The Edgeley road.

4 Lakey Hill.

5 Joe Grundy's pasture.

6 Lower Loxley.

7 Arkwright Lake.

8 The Berrow Estate.

9 Darrington.

10 You'd go from Paddington to Hollerton Junction.

11 Heydon Berrow. Black Lawson gallops across the Berrow on Lady Day, accompanied by two hell-hounds, or so Joe Grundy says.

12 Wharton's Garage.

HOW OLD ARE THEY?

Arrange the following characters in age order, the oldest first:

1 Lilian Bellamy.

2 Jennifer Aldridge.

3 Tony Archer.

4 Walter Gabriel.

5 Adam Macy.

6 Elizabeth Archer.

7 Joe Grundy.

8 Lucy Perks.

9 Phil Archer.

10 Tom Forrest.

11 Thomas Archer.

12 Shula Hebden.

A HOW OLD ARE THEY?

The ages given are as at 1 March, 1988:

1 Walter Gabriel (91).

2 Tom Forrest (77).

3 Joe Grundy (66).

4 Phil Archer (59).

5 Jennifer Aldridge (43).

6 Lilian Bellamy (40).

7 Tony Archer (37).

8 Shula Hebden (29).

9 Elizabeth Archer (20).

10 Adam Macy (20).

11 Lucy Perks (16).

12 Thomas Archer (7).

ARRIVALS

1 Who arrived in a mysterious green caravan?

2 Where did the Snells live before moving to Ambridge?

3 Why did Neil Carter move to the village?

4 When Sid Perks first arrived in Ambridge, who spotted his potential and gave him a job?

5 Who made a triumphant return to Ambridge accompanied by Dan and Phil and the Hollerton Silver Band?

6 Who moved into the Grey Gables Country Club in 1962?

7 What means of transport does Mrs Walker use to get to her clients?

8 Who arrived at home very suddenly after her expulsion from school?

9 Where did the Frys live on their arrival in Ambridge in 1988?

10 Who ran a wine bar in Bristol before working in Ambridge?

11 Who was the first to arrive at the scene when Bob Larkin was shot during a struggle with Tom?

12 Pat's uncle arrived in Ambridge and ruffled feathers when he proved more of a dab hand at something than the locals? What was he so good at?

A ARRIVALS

1 John Tregorran.

2 Sunningdale.

3 He was a 'new entrant', or trainee, at Brookfield.

4 Fellow Brummie, Jack Woolley.

5 Tom Forrest after his acquittal of the manslaughter of Bob Larkin.

6 Jack Woolley.

7 Moped.

8 Elizabeth Archer.

9 Woodbine Cottage.

10 Caroline Bone.

11 Phil.

12 Bowls. Ewan Llewellyn won the local tournament, but was persuaded to leave the trophy in The Bull rather than take it back to Wales.

WEDDINGS

1 Who gave Phil and Jill a car as a wedding present?

2 In what year did Mark and Shula marry?

3 Who were the two bridesmaids when Sid Perks married Polly Mead?

4 Tom Forrest married late in life. In what year?

5 Who asked an Ambridge farmer to marry her? He accepted the offer with some alacrity, by the way.

6 Who made the bridesmaids' dresses for Mark and Shula's wedding?

7 Who married in a registry office in 1987 with strangers as witnesses?

8 Who so disagreed with his daughter's marriage that at first he refused to give her away – although he relented before the wedding?

9 Phil (then a widower) and John Tregorran made a cine-film together of a family wedding. Whose?

10 Where did Phil propose to Jill?

11 Who tried to move the date of his wedding because he'd been told there would be tax advantages in doing so?

12 Which divorcé married in St Stephen's amid considerable controversy?

A WEDDINGS

1 George Fairbrother, father of Phil's first wife.

2 1985.

3 Lilian and Jennifer Archer.

4 1958.

5 Pat proposed to Tony Archer.

6 Sophie Barlow.

7 Sid and Kathy Perks.

8 Jethro Larkin. He didn't think Eddie was good enough for Clarrie and many would still agree with him.

9 The wedding of Christine Archer and Paul Johnson.

10 New Street Station, Birmingham.

11 Phil, when he was marrying Grace. She was hurt by the idea and the ceremony took place on Easter Monday as planned.

12 George Barford, to Christine Johnson.

ANIMALS

1 Caroline Bone first arrived at The Bull with what sort of dog in tow?

2 When she first moved to Grey Gables, another boisterous dog was to dominate Caroline's life. What breed this time?

3 Who shot Charlie?

4 What prize did Captain win at the village fête?

5 What traditional beverage did Jethro and his dog Gyp take in the afternoon?

6 Midnight was the horse Grace rushed into that fatal fire to save . . . Midnight was Christine's horse. Who originally gave him to her?

7 Who trained his sheepdog, Nell, during his retirement?

8 Who were Daisy and Heidi?

9 If you find a baby deer you should leave it, as its mother will probably return. Why then, did Caroline Bone hand-rear Doughnut, the fawn she found?

10 Who bought Jethro his dog, Gyp?

11 Which animal brought Susan and Neil Carter together?

12 From where did Laura Archer obtain Jessica, the hen?

ANIMALS

1. A great dane called Leo. He was such a nuisance that Walter had to give him some of his granny's embrocation to make him sleep while Caroline worked.

2. Charlie the old english sheepdog.

3. Mike Tucker, believing him to be sheep-worrying.

4. 'Dog most like its master'.

5. They always took tea together.

6. He was a birthday present from Dan, and cost 60 guineas.

7. Dan.

8. Laura Archer's goats, and how she doted on them.

9. Its mother had been killed by poachers in the Country Park.

10. Phil.

11. Pinky the pig. Susan won him in the village fête. She had to ask Neil's advice on pig husbandry and romance blossomed.

12. She was a battery hen from Neil's unit. Laura was appalled at her condition and nursed her back to health.

Q AMBRIDGE GARDENS (1)

1 Dan Archer's delphiniums were his pride and joy, but each year he had to protect them against which garden pests in particular?

2 What is the name of the Aldridges' gardener?

3 Tom Forrest 'chits' his potato tubers before planting to ensure he has the earliest potatoes in Ambridge. What is 'chitting'?

4 Ever since Dan gave Doris a bunch of St John's wort in their courting days, it was her favourite flower. What colour is the bloom?

5 Peggy grows Gardener's Delight. What is this?

6 Martha Woodford was caught digging up primroses in Leaders Wood to transplant them to her garden. Was Mrs Antrobus correct to warn her that this is against the law?

7 Lynda Snell calls this hardy flower nigella. What does everyone else in Ambridge call it?

8 Why does Jack Woolley need a stiff drink when he hears the word 'thrips'?

9 Pat's garden contains these herbs. What are they?
   a looks like grass, tastes like a mild onion and has purple flowers.
   b a bushy shrub with small blue flowers, narrow leaves, used for seasoning lamb.
   c strong flavoured, soft leaved and used with onion for stuffing.
   d a vigorous spreading perennial, best with new potatoes and peas.

A AMBRIDGE GARDENS (1)

1 Slugs and snails. They just love young delphinium shoots.

2 Mr Walker, husband of Jennifer's terrifying cleaner.

3 Tom stores them in the light from January until March, allowing them to sprout before planting.

4 Yellow.

5 A delicious variety of small tomato.

6 Yes, but she is allowed to take them away with the owner's permission.

7 Love-in-a-mist. Sometimes it is known as devil-in-a-bush. The pretty blue (or occasionally white) flowers are visible through feathery foliage.

8 These are pests which can attack the buds and blooms of greenhouse-grown chrysanthemums.

9 a chives
   b rosemary
   c sage
   d mint

DEATHS

1 What farm animal did Phil recently receive on the death of a local farmer?

2 A cow died of bloat when Ruth was left in charge at Brookfield. What is bloat?

3 Paul Johnson, Christine's first husband, died abroad after their separation. Where did he die?

4 Who played 'Death' in Mrs Antrobus' morality play, an entertainment scheduled to replace the Christmas review one year?

5 Two villagers have died in car crashes near Ambridge. Can you name them?

6 Who was with Dan Archer when he died?

7 Who was with Jethro Larkin when he died?

8 When did Jack Archer die?

9 Grace Archer died in a fire at Grey Gables. It was Grace who discovered that fire. How?

10 Letty Lawson-Hope left Doris something in her will. What?

11 Who was reported to have died in a plane crash – and reappeared in Borchester the following year?

12 Whose father died of lung cancer?

A DEATHS

1 Freda, a rare breed of pig.

2 The animal swells up due to a build-up of gasses in the rumen.

3 Germany.

4 Joe Grundy. He was chosen, said Eddie, because he wouldn't need any make-up for the part.

5 Polly Perks and Janet Tregorran.

6 His granddaughter Elizabeth.

7 David Archer. They were lopping a tree together when a branch fell on Jethro.

8 January 1982.

9 She and Phil were having a drink when she realised she had lost an ear-ring. She went back to the car to find it and saw the fire.

10 Glebe Cottage – but it was for Doris' lifetime only. To secure the cottage in perpetuity, Doris later had to pay the Lawson-Hope estate a nominal sum.

11 Nelson Gabriel. His reappearance was at Borchester Assizes, charged with a mail van robbery.

12 Nigel Pargetter's father.

THE WORLD OUTSIDE (1)

Life goes on in Ambridge, often oblivious to the world events that are taking place elsewhere. Can you match the comparatively trivial events in Ambridge (a to l) with what was happening in the world outside at the same time (1 to 12)?

Ambridge events

a   Jack Woolley buys Grenville's estate.

b   Mark is at loggerheads over a court case with his girlfriend's father: Phil.

c   Christine Archer refuses Clive Lawson-Hope's proposal.

d   Jill and Phil get engaged.

e   George Fairbrother sells the estate to Grenville.

f   There are intruders at Brookfield and Doris is injured.

g   Tony meets Pat.

h   Shula and Neil sit on Lakey Hill most of the night watching the Jubilee bonfires stretch into the distance.

i   Eddie Grundy buys a new Capri with a Colonel Bogey horn.

j   Clive Lawson-Hope, son of the squire, proposes to Grace Fairbrother.

k   Lilian falls in love with a Canadian Air Force pilot.

1   Dan asks Phil if his future plans include farming
     Brookfield: and is told they don't.

World events

1   The death of Stalin.

2   The election of Kurt Waldheim as president of
    Austria.

3   The Paris student riots.

4   Dr Christiaan Barnard performs the first heart
    transplant.

5   Roger Bannister runs the first four-minute-mile.

6   Spain holds its first free parliamentary elections
    since Franco's rise to power.

7   The USSR launches Sputnik.

8   Fidel Castro becomes president of Cuba.

9   Richard Nixon resigns as president of the USA
    after Watergate.

10 The Suez Crisis.

11 US aircraft bomb North Vietnam and the action
    escalates into war.

12 Ronald Reagan is elected president of the USA for
    the first time.

A THE WORLD OUTSIDE (1)

1   j   (March 1953).
2   i   (April 1986).
3   k   (May 1968).
4   f   (December 1967).
5   c   (May 1954).
6   h   (June 1977).
7   d   (October 1957).
8   e   (January 1959).
9   g   (August 1974).
10 l   (November 1956).
11 a   (February 1965).
12 b   (November 1980).

GENERAL QUESTIONS (3)

1 Which otherwise respectable couple was caught watching television without a licence in 1978?

2 Which Archer was admitted to mental hospital in 1954?

3 To whom did Mrs Fairbrother sell the estate after her husband's death?

4 In 1967 Phil won a competition in a farming paper. What was the very exciting prize?

5 When did the Ambridge village school close? Was it in 1960, 1973 or 1980?

6 Who bottled too much fruit one year, gave the excess to her friends, and was accused of using the fruit to 'buy' votes in the WI election?

7 What have Jolene Rogers and Dolly Treadgold in common?

8 Who is editor of the parish magazine?

9 Who disliked the Series Three communion service so much that she went to Evensong instead of Family Communion?

10 Why did Peggy and Jack Archer leave their smallholding in Cornwall so abruptly?

11 Who lived together as landlady and lodger for many years, having decided they were happier that way than as man and wife?

12 How does Martha Woodford get to the shop every day from her cottage?

A GENERAL QUESTIONS (3)

1 Freddie Danby and Laura Archer. They escaped without a fine, but had to buy a backdated licence.

2 Jack Archer.

3 Charles Grenville.

4 A three-month tour of farms in the USA, Canada, New Zealand and Australia.

5 1973, amid much opposition.

6 Doris. As if she would do such a thing.

7 They are both former girlfriends of Eddie Grundy.

8 Mrs Marjorie Antrobus.

9 Doris Archer.

10 Jack's partner and old army chum, Barney Lee, was getting too fond of Peggy.

11 Laura Archer and Colonel Freddie Danby.

12 By bicycle.

THE CHURCH

1 Who was Richard Adamson's predecessor as vicar of Ambridge? And who was *his* predecessor?

2 Where did David and Sophie plan to marry – until they agreed not to go ahead with the wedding?

3 Joe Grundy left the Church of England to join which Church?

4 What was the issue over which Joe and Richard Adamson could not agree, which made Joe leave the Anglican Church?

5 To whom is the church at Ambridge dedicated?

6 If you think that one was too easy, to whom is the church at Penny Hassett dedicated?

7 Who are the churchwardens in Ambridge?

8 Nigel Pargetter made a sponsored parachute jump (David offered to double his sponsorship if Nigel didn't open his parachute) in aid of which good cause?

9 At which church did Phil and Jill marry?

10 Name the Bishop of Felpersham.

11 Which family memorial – big as a bus and sadly chipped by David's digger – stands in Ambridge churchyard?

12 When was the Ambridge vicarage built?

A THE CHURCH

1   David Latimer was vicar of Ambridge from 1968 to 1973 and Matthew Wrefford 1961 to 1968.

2   Felpersham Cathedral.

3   Methodist. However, after the Bishop of Felpersham visited Grange Farm and found himself on first name terms with the Grundys, Joe decided the Anglicans weren't so bad.

4   Richard said that the story of Noah's flood was not to be taken literally – and Joe thought it was.

5   St Stephen.

6   St Saviour.

7   Jill Archer and Tom Forrest.

8   The church organ fund.

9   Crudley church. This is the only time Jill's home village has been featured in *The Archers*.

10 Cyril.

11 The Lawson-Hope Memorial.

12 1975, soon after the Adamsons arrived in the village. The old vicarage was sold by the Church.

Q QUESTIONS FOR NEW LISTENERS

1 Which county cricket team played a charity match against South Borset in 1988?

2 Where did Elizabeth go for six months of sun and surf?

3 Who was the first person Elizabeth met on her unexpected return?

4 Mrs Walker rearranged her other ladies so that she could spend most of her week cleaning where?

5 What new venture did Pat and Tony attempt in the autumn of 1988?

6 Who moved in with Caroline and Matthew while renovations were carried out at home?

7 Nigel's house is in poor condition, but which part of it is in special need of repair?

8 What were Phil and Jill worried to learn about David's new girlfriend, Frances?

9 Jill calls at Walter Gabriel's with something warm several days a week? What is it?

10 Joe and Eddie promised to get her old one repaired, but Clarrie bought a brand new one. What is it?

11 After the fire at the barn conversions, treasure seekers and scavengers moved in. What did the Grundys take from the site?

12 Which conservation project at Home Farm did Lynda Snell become closely involved with?

A QUESTIONS FOR NEW LISTENERS

1 Worcestershire – but Ambridge players were excluded from the South Borset side.

2 Australia.

3 Bert Fry, then unknown to her.

4 Lower Loxley Hall, stately pile of the Pargetters.

5 The manufacture and sale of organic yoghurt.

6 Nelson Gabriel.

7 The rotting staircase.

8 She was divorced with two children.

9 His meal on wheels.

10 A fully automatic washing machine.

11 A pink bidet. Clarrie told Joe to take it back in case it was haunted, like the house.

12 Brian's farm pool.

SICKNESS AND HEALTH (1)

1 Who passed out after giving blood when the mobile transfusion unit came to Ambridge?

2 Who, in 1959, fell from the roof of the implement shed on to the binder, fracturing his leg and a rib?

3 Which villager is a martyr to her hip and cannot walk unaided?

4 Ruth, the Brookfield student, was rushed to casualty when a bone in her foot was thought to have broken. How did this happen?

5 Jack Woolley left hospital in 1988 with something he didn't have when admitted. What?

6 Dr Thorogood is Ambridge's GP but he also works shifts at Borchester General. In which department?

7 Who did Dr Thorogood wrongfully accuse of stealing the key to his dispensary?

8 Which Ambridge child was bitten by an adder and was only saved by a new Yugoslavian snake serum?

9 Which Ambridge child spent a night in hospital after misbehaving at a fireworks party?

10 Who died in 1976 when an aluminium ladder he was carrying touched an overhead power cable?

11 Jack Woolley had a heart attack in 1973 after receiving some bad news. What was it?

12 Sid collapsed in The Bull in 1985 and spent two weeks in hospital. What was wrong with him?

A SICKNESS AND HEALTH (1)

1 Sid Perks.

2 Dan Archer.

3 Mrs Potter, never heard but often spoken of.

4 A cow stood on her foot. In fact, it was only bruised.

5 A pacemaker.

6 Casualty.

7 Lucy Perks, who had been in the surgery that day with her green-haired chum Art.

8 Adam Macy.

9 Once again, the accident-prone Adam Macy.

10 Arthur Tovey, the manager of Carol Tregorran's orchards.

11 Valerie wanted a divorce.

12 He had a perforated ulcer, a condition which seemed to confirm the villagers' belief that Sid wasn't looking after himself properly.

PLACES

1 What became of Arkwright Hall?

2 Which housing scheme did Jack Woolley mastermind in the late 1970s, against much local opposition?

3 Where was Duckingham Palace?

4 Who worked at The Bull as a barmaid, and became licensee eight years later?

5 A consortium of businessmen were interested in building a housing estate in Ambridge in 1987. To which village was the consortium persuaded to shift its interest?

6 Where is the nearest racecourse to Ambridge?

7 Of which company is Sir Sidney Goodman the chairman?

8 Where does Mrs Antrobus live?

9 To which county did the vicar and his wife, Richard and Dorothy Adamson, move?

10 Which family has lived at Willow Farm twice?

11 At which restaurant did the Archers celebrate Phil's sixtieth birthday?

12 Which farmhouse became a doctor's home and surgery?

A | PLACES

1. It was turned into a Field Studies Centre in the early 1970s and has scarcely been mentioned again.

2. Glebelands.

3. The shed in the garden of Ambridge Hall where Laura Archer kept her ducks.

4. Polly Mead. She was Polly Perks when she was licensee.

5. Edgeley.

6. Felpersham.

7. The Borchester Canning Factory.

8. Nightingale Farm.

9. County Durham.

10. The Tuckers.

11. The Apple Tree, in Felpersham.

12. Ambridge Farmhouse, home of the Tuckers.

TECHNOLOGY AND THE UNEXPLAINED

1 Who bought one of the first TV sets in Ambridge and had a party at Brookfield to celebrate?

2 What sort of ghost is said to haunt The Bull?

3 Who was convinced, when ITV was launched, that it would never be watched at Brookfield?

4 Which of the houses formed by the barn conversions remained unsold after rumours that it was haunted?

5 Even Mark thought he saw something moving in the barn conversions. What had he seen?

6 What did Tom Forrest and Lynda Snell find in the rubble of the barn conversions which seemed to vindicate Lynda's ghostly theories?

7 Who had a computer for her birthday which was rapidly used by the bell-ringers to work a new variation into the 'Grandsire Doubles'?

8 Who refused to believe that the smudge on a photo of her cottage was bonfire smoke and not a ghost?

9 What did Phil's family give him for his sixtieth birthday?

10 Who restored an Edison standard phonograph to order in 1976?

11 In 1983 villagers thought they saw a hob-hound. After the death of a number of sheep, what was revealed as the hob-hound's real identity?

12 Who was annoyed to discover that one of the farm workers had bought a TV set before the farmer?

TECHNOLOGY AND THE UNEXPLAINED

1   Mrs Perkins, not normally noted for her go-ahead ideas.

2   A little drummer-boy from the Civil War.

3   Christine Archer, in a rare bit of flag-waving for the BBC.

4   The small one, originally intended for Sophie and David to live in, had their marriage taken place.

5   A crow which had fallen down the chimney.

6   A coin dating from the Civil War – the ghost was also alleged to date from this time.

7   Lucy Perks, for her eleventh birthday.

8   Polly Perks. The photo was taken while Rose Cottage was being renovated.

9   A personal computer.

10 Walter Gabriel.

11 It was a lynx.

12 Doris. She resolved to persuade Dan to buy one at once, but discovered he had already ordered a set.

FARMING (2)

1 Caroline Bone can remember hunting over stubble all winter. These days, the ground has usually been cultivated before the hunting season starts. Why?

2 Brian Aldridge is a member of both the NFU and the CLA. What are these two organisations?

3 In January 1988, who was working at Brookfield Farm?

4 To whom do the Ambridge dairy farmers sell their milk?

5 David's on the combine, Ruth's on the tractor and Phil's double-checking that the grain is dry enough for the first cut of the harvest. Which cereal?

6 On which farm did Arthur work?

7 What crop turns Brian's fields yellow in May?

8 Tony Archer was furious to catch children sliding down a mountain of black polythene sheeting held down by tyres. What were they sliding down, and why was Tony angry?

9 At Brookfield, lambing starts at the end of February. So when does tupping (putting the ewes to the ram) take place?

10 What do Simon, Ned, Jethro and Len all have in common?

11 When Neil Carter can't take part in a darts match, his team mates forgive him because he explains that a gilt is farrowing. What does he mean?

12 Who in Ambridge sells Christmas turkeys?

A FARMING (2)

1 Most cereals are now wintersown instead of springsown. So, as soon as one crop is out of the ground, the next crop is usually drilled.

2 The National Farmers' Union (which represents the interests of both tenant farmers and landowning farmers), and the Country Landowners' Association (which represents the interests of landowners only).

3 Phil, David, Graham Collard, Ruth Pritchard and Neil Carter.

4 The Milk Marketing Board.

5 Winter barley ripens before wheat.

6 Bridge Farm. He was Pat and Tony's YTS worker.

7 Oilseed rape.

8 A silage clamp, a common sight on British farms now. When the sheeting is pulled back, the smell can be pungent.

9 October. Ewes carry their lambs for about five months.

10 They were all workers at Brookfield.

11 A pig is about to have her first litter.

12 The Grundys.

GENERAL QUESTIONS (4)

1 Dan had two brothers: can you name them?

2 What gadget was Jill demonstrating in Borchester when Phil caught sight of her for almost the first time?

3 In 1972 Jack Woolley introduced deer to the park of Grey Gables and something infinitely heavier. What?

4 Why was Kenton not heard for many years, until 1988?

5 Which A level did David fail twice, much to his father's fury?

6 Where did Elizabeth Archer go to school when she failed her entrance exams to Borchester Grammar.

7 In 1982 Phil and Jill returned from Hong Kong to walk straight into a party organised for them to celebrate what?

8 Who won the 1984 Ambridge treasure hunt?

9 Whom did smooth-talking Mike Daly dub 'the lily of Ambridge'?

10 The Bull had a new piano in 1983. Why?

11 When was the Ambridge Millenium Festival?

12 When Phil Archer JP found Mark's clients guilty, Mark sent a statement to the *Borchester Echo* condemning the local magistrates. What was the issue at stake?

A GENERAL QUESTIONS (4)

1   John and Frank. Frank went to New Zealand and John to Canada.

2   The House Drudge was the name of the gadget, and Jill jokes that this is subsequently exactly what she became.

3   The Empress of Ambridge, an old steam engine.

4   He was always away, bobbing around on the high seas with the Merchant Navy.

5   Maths.

6   Cherrington, a boarding school about 50 miles from Ambridge.

7   Their silver wedding anniversary.

8   Eddie Grundy. Nelson discovered the booty but Eddie's ferret, Tex, was lurking in the same spot and Eddie was the first to touch the treasure.

9   Mrs Perkins. Well I warned you he was smooth-talking.

10 Eddie Grundy had ruined the old one by being sick in it and so the Grundys replaced it.

11 1973. It included plays, sports and a garden competition, organised by Doris.

12 Hunting. Mark's clients were hunt saboteurs and the magistrates had found them guilty of criminal damage.

Q PRIVATE ENTERPRISE (2)

1 Christine Archer and Grace Fairbrother set up a business together in 1952. What was it?

2 Who tried to cash in on the building of the Borchester bypass in 1960 by starting his own haulage business?

3 When Elizabeth Archer tried to run a fashion business, Jill ended up doing most of the work. Who helped by doing Jill's housework?

4 With whom did Elizabeth run the business?

5 Which villager owned an antique shop in Borchester long before Nelson Gabriel?

6 Who was Ambridge's baker for ten years from the mid-1950s to the mid-1960s?

7 What was Betty's Barn?

8 Who worked for John Tregorran in his bookshop and eventually became a partner?

9 What business did Haydn Evans buy from Ralph Bellamy in 1975?

10 Why did Paul Johnson's fish farm run into trouble?

11 What scheme was run jointly between Jack Woolley and Christine Johnson in 1980?

12 What was The Two Jays Craft Studio?

A PRIVATE ENTERPRISE (2)

1 A riding school.

2 Jack Archer. Like most Ambridge enterprises, it didn't last long.

3 Nigel Pargetter.

4 Sophie Barlow, David's fiancée.

5 John Tregorran. Carol put up some of the money.

6 Doughy Hood.

7 The Tuckers' farm shop. It was open for business for just three months, in 1984.

8 Roger Travers-Macy.

9 The village garage.

10 The trout died when the water filter broke – and Paul had cut costs by not taking out any insurance.

11 Riding holidays, including accommodation at Grey Gables.

12 A venture set up in the 1970s by Jill and Jennifer, the two Js concerned. It was doomed to failure.

MORE SPORTS

1   Who fell off his horse at the opening meet of the South Borsetshire Hunt into Phil Archer's winter barley?

2   In the early 1970s, Sid Perks organised a football team in the village. What was the team called?

3   Whose racehorse was Grey Silk?

4   Who has been a consistent opponent of blood sports for the last thirty years?

5   Jack Woolley's swimming pool should have had Bath stone laid all around it. What was actually laid, and had to be hastily replaced?

6   Bowls enjoyed a fifteen-year vogue in Ambridge. Who was responsible for starting the idea in 1953?

7   Where is the Ambridge cricket pitch?

8   When the new cricket pavilion was opened in 1983, against which team did Ambridge play the opening match?

9   What is the name of the coveted shield presented to the winners of the South Borsetshire Village Cricket League?

10 In 1975 a historic football match ended in a draw. Who were Ambridge Wanderers' opponents? Clue: Pat Archer was captain of the team.

11 Who is currently captain of The Bull darts team?

12 Why did Sid Perks have to give barmaid Jackie Smith a day off when the Hunt met at The Bull?

A MORE SPORTS

1 Nigel Pargetter.

2 Ambridge Wanderers. They didn't wander much further than Edgeley.

3 Jack Woolley's, given him in settlement of a debt in 1975. Ralph Bellamy shared in the running costs but Grey Silk had an undistinguished career.

4 Jill Archer.

5 Crazy paving.

6 Jack Archer.

7 Grey Gables, by kind permission of Jack Woolley. It moved from the village green in 1982.

8 Penny Hassett.

9 The Netherbourne Shield.

10 A ladies' football team, started by Harry Booker.

11 Neil Carter.

12 She strongly disagreed with blood sports.

Q SCANDALS

1 Shortly before she was due to leave her farm, what did Mary Pound reveal about her marriage to Ken?

2 Who saw Brian kissing Caroline in the Country Park?

3 Irish farmworker Paddy Redmond was the father of Jennifer's illegitimate baby: to whom was he engaged at the time?

4 Why did Brian Aldridge run into serious trouble with the Farm Workers' Union?

5 With whom was Pat Archer suspected of having an affair in 1984?

6 With whom was Jennifer accused of having an affair, both by her husband and many villagers?

7 Why did Betty Tucker leave her job at Home Farm?

8 Who at Grange Farm was so scared by Eddie's advances that she stayed in her room most of the time?

9 While Pat was away, Tony was spotted more than once with flirtatious Libby Jones, whose job involved visiting the farm. What was her job?

10 Who promised not to tell his boss about his colleague's alcoholism?

11 Mrs Antrobus banned a shocking double act from the village Christmas revue. What were Nigel Pargetter and Matthew Thorogood planning to do?

12 Who feared that his son's drunken and criminal behaviour was caused by his own broken marriage?

SCANDALS

1 That she'd had an affair with one Silas Winter, who was really the father of her daughter Marilyn.

2 Tony Archer, but no one would believe his scandalous story.

3 Barmaid Nora McAuley.

4 He hit a worker, Jack Roberts. Roberts was sacked and later lost his unfair dismissal case against Brian.

5 Roger, a lecturer at Borchester Tech who obviously took his Women's Studies class seriously.

6 John Tregorran.

7 Because her husband found out that she had been forced to fight off Brian Aldridge's lustful advances.

8 The young nursery nurse who arrived to help Clarrie after the birth of Edward. Her name was Samantha Walton.

9 Milk recorder.

10 Tom Forrest. The alcoholic was George Barford.

11 Imitate Jack Woolley grovelling to Prince Charles.

12 George Barford. Terry later made good in the Prince of Wales' Own Regiment of Yorkshire.

Q MORE DEATHS

1   In what year did Dan die?

2   Who left 8 acres to George Barford?

3   How did Paul Johnson, Christine's estranged husband, die?

4   Where was Dan when Christine came to break the news of Doris' death?

5   What were Dan's last words to Elizabeth?

6   What was Joby Woodford doing when he died?

7   The congregation at Doris' funeral sang her favourite psalm. What was it?

8   Who forgot to sign her will, so that her property did not go to whom she intended?

9   Doris Archer died peacefully in an armchair at Brookfield. Who found her?

10 Where did Jack Archer die?

11 Phil was left with a tax bill to pay after Dan's death. How did he raise the necessary £50 000?

12 Who decided to open his house to the public when his father died?

A MORE DEATHS

1   1986.

2   Bill Insley, who had been share-farming with Neil.

3   In an accident on the autobahn.

4   At the church.

5   He told her to be a good girl.

6   Helping Martha stocktake in the shop.

7   Psalm 121: 'I will lift up mine eyes unto the hills.'

8   Laura Archer. She thought she had left Ambridge Hall to Freddie Danby.

9   Shula.

10 In a sanitorium in Scotland.

11 By selling off some land, part of it to the developers who carried out the barn conversions.

12 Nigel Pargetter, in a bid to make some money which would pay for repairs.

Q FARMING (3)

1 Dan Archer went to market and bought six sheep for £7 10s. Can you guess when this might have been. Was it in 1951, 1956 or 1964?

2 In which year did Dan, still reluctant to retire, at least agree to move out of Brookfield so that Phil and Jill could move in?

3 What was Dan doing when he suffered from his fatal heart attack?

4 Phil knew he needed more money to marry Grace so their relationship depended on the success of which specialist area of the farm?

5 What name is always given to the boar in Phil's pig unit at Hollowtree?

6 Which big agricultural event, held at the beginning of July, does Phil usually try to attend?

7 Which big agricultural event, held at the beginning of December, does Brian usually try to attend?

8 Where did David Archer go to learn more about agriculture after leaving college and before starting work at Brookfield?

9 What crisis in 1986 wiped out many of Brookfield's lambs?

10 To most farmers leatherjackets aren't something to wear. What are they?

11 How can Brian tell the age of his stags at a glance?

12 Tony has some 'store' cattle. What are they?

A FARMING (3)

1 1956: ewes were especially cheap that year.

2 1969, although Phil and Jill didn't move in until the following year.

3 Picking up a sheep which was on its back. Ewes often get stuck when they are carrying a lot of wool.

4 The new pig unit. While following the romance of Grace and Phil, the nation learned a great deal about pigs.

5 Playboy.

6 The Royal Show, held at Stoneleigh in Warwickshire.

7 Smithfield Show, held at Earl's Court.

8 The Netherlands.

9 An abortion infection attacked the flock.

10 Larvae of the crane-fly or daddy-long-legs, which can damage grassland badly.

11 By the size of their antlers. The older the stag, the greater the size and number of branches.

12 Beasts (in Tony's case, cattle) which are well grown but still need fattening before slaughter.

Q ASSOCIATIONS

With whom do you associate the following?

1 Cans of lager?

2 A clapped-out Spitfire, Radio 3 roaring from the stereo?

3 A hostess trolley?

4 Chutney, bottled fruits, jams and preserves?

5 A nodding ferret in the back window of the Capri?

6 The motorway to Birmingham?

7 An Aga.

8 Home-made parsnip wine?

9 An XR3i?

10 A pipe?

11 Farmers' lung?

12 Borchester Womens' Group?

ASSOCIATIONS

1 Tony Archer.

2 Colonel Danby. He bought the Spitfire from David.

3 Walter. He tried to get rid of it, but Nelson bought it a second time.

4 Pru. She spends so much time making all this that she is seldom heard.

5 Eddie Grundy.

6 Commuter Mark Hebden.

7 Jill.

8 Martha. Said wine spelt the downfall of Colonel Danby.

9 David, Phil gave him one.

10 Bert Fry now, but for many years Walter was a pipe-smoker.

11 Joe Grundy.

12 Pat Archer.

FIRES

1   Who was missing and presumed dead after a fire at Peggy Archer's Blossom Hill Cottage?

2   In what year did the village hall catch fire?

3   In 1959 which of Walter's friends fought a fire in his workshop?

4   In the 1960s, a known arsonist was admitted to mental hospital. Who is his granddaughter?

5   What, to the relief of all the locals, caught fire at The Bull after Sid's attempts to repair it?

6   Where were the Tregorrans living when fire struck their home – and John realised they were uninsured?

7   There was a fire at Brookfield in 1966. Who caused it?

8   Where was the fire in which Grace died?

9   In which year did this historic event take place?

10 Who fought the fire as soon as it was discovered?

11 Where did Grace die?

12 Who was with her?

FIRES

1 Sammy the cat. How he can have escaped from the fire remains a mystery to this day.

2 1976.

3 Tom Forrest and Mrs Perkins. The latter admonished Walter because he didn't seem grateful enough for this noble act.

4 Lucy Perks. The arsonist was Frank Mead, her maternal grandfather.

5 A TV set that Sid had tried to introduce to the bar. Nora fought the blaze stoutly, but to no avail.

6 Manor Court. They moved back to this house after it was repaired in 1970.

7 Frank Mead.

8 The stables at Grey Gables.

9 September, 1955.

10 Phil, Grace, Reggie, Valerie, John Tregorran and Carol Grey. Soon after, Dan, Tom and Walter arrived.

11 In the ambulance.

12 Phil. She died in his arms on the way to hospital.

THE WORLD OUTSIDE (2)

Can you match the comparatively trivial events in Ambridge (a to l) with what was happening in the world outside at the same time (1 to 12)?

Ambridge events

a   Smallholder Carol Grey is engaged to the new squire, Charles Grenville.

b   The Borchester bypass threatens the Fairbrother estate.

c   Dan's pigs catch swine fever.

d   John Tregorran mourns the death of his wife, Janet.

e   Tom and Pru Forrest decide to become foster parents.

f   Nelson flirts with Christine Archer and is warned off by her fiancé.

g   Jack Archer plans to revamp The Bull with fruit machines and expresso coffee.

h   Elizabeth fails the entrance exams for Borchester Grammar.

i   Shula returns from Bangkok.

j   Chris and George Barford are married.

k   Laura Archer arrives at Brookfield.

l   Shula decides to leave Brookfield for Asia and New Zealand.

World events

1 Neil Armstrong and Buzz Aldrin land on the moon.

2 Mother Teresa is awarded the Nobel Peace Prize.

3 Edmund Hillary and Sherpa Tenzing climb Everest.

4 The first Aldermaston march is held by CND to protest against nuclear arms.

5 President Kennedy is assassinated by Lee Harvey Oswald.

6 Mrs Thatcher is elected prime minister for the first time.

7 The Berlin Wall is constructed.

8 The first premium bonds are drawn.

9 The Camp David peace agreement is signed by Prime Minister Begin and President Sadat.

10 Khrushchev comes to power in Russia.

11 Sixty-seven demonstrators are shot in Sharpeville, South Africa.

12 Ayatollah Khomeni returns to Iran to head the Islamic revolution.

A THE WORLD OUTSIDE (2)

1   g   (July 1969).
2   i   (October 1979).
3   c   (May 1953).
4   f   (August 1956).
5   d   (November 1963).
6   l   (May 1979).
7   a   (August 1961).
8   k   (June 1957).
9   j   (March 1979).
10   b   (March 1958).
11   e   (March 1960).
12   h   (February 1979).

GENERAL QUESTIONS (5)

1 Has Ambridge ever won the best kept village competition?

2 Name the estate agency that Shula works for.

3 What is the name of the rival agency in Borchester?

4 Jill Archer is a proud and upstanding member of the WRVS. What do these initials stand for?

5 Who felt professionally snubbed when the wooden chairs in the garden of The Bull were replaced by plastic ones?

6 With which family was Doris in service in her youth?

7 After whom did Matthew Thorogood name his dog?

8 Who was married to both the men who have run Grey Gables?

9 Which band regularly entertains the diners at Grey Gables?

10 Phil wanted the twins to be educated privately, Jill wanted them to go to the village school. Who won this battle?

11 What have Eric Selwyn, Bill Morris and Simon Parker got in common?

12 Jethro was furious with Clarrie when she asked Phil to make improvements to Woodbine Cottage. What, in particular did she request?

A GENERAL QUESTIONS (5)

1 No. In 1975 and 1987 Ambridge was second, failing to win in 1987 because the Loxley Barratt Morris Men threw their unsightly beer cans in the pond.

2 Rodway and Watson.

3 Drinkwaters.

4 Womens' Royal Voluntary Service.

5 Woodman Joby Woodford. He would have liked to make Sid and Polly some rustic furniture.

6 The Lawson-Hopes.

7 Cole Porter.

8 Valerie Grayson first married Reggie Trentham and then Jack Woolley.

9 The Tommy Croaker Quartet.

10 Jill.

11 They are all former boyfriends of Shula.

12 A modernised kitchen, in particular a new range.

OTHER PLACES

1 Kathy drove Sid and Lucy to their holiday destination when Sid came out of hospital. Where was it?

2 Shortly before his death, Jethro planned a wonderful long-haul holiday to stay with an old friend. What was Jethro's intended destination?

3 Devoted father Walter Gabriel went where, in the 1950s, to be with Nelson while he was in hospital?

4 Where did Mrs Perkins and Arthur get married?

5 Where does Sid Perks come from?

6 Sid and Polly Perks, unusually, went on holiday with Dan and Doris Archer in 1967. Where to?

7 On a village trip to Holland, what sport did Ambridge play successfully against the Dutch?

8 Who recently went on a trip to Florence?

9 While travelling in the USA, John Tregorran discovered a small town called Ambridge. Which state is it in?

10 In the 1950s, Christine was befriended by the rather domineering Lady Hyleberrow. Where did she ask Chris to travel with her? Was it to Ethiopia, Cheltenham or Provence?

11 Where did Paul Johnson live after his separation from Christine?

12 In 1979 Phil and Jill received an alarming telephone call from Shula at the British Embassy in Bangkok. Why did she call them?

A OTHER PLACES

1 Lyme Regis.

2 Canada.

3 Southampton.

4 On a cruise, destination unspecified.

5 Birmingham.

6 Scotland.

7 Bowls.

8 Mark, Shula, Matthew and Caroline. Mark and Caroline drank in the culture while Matthew and Shula preferred the Chianti.

9 Pennsylvania.

10 Ethiopia. Dan wanted to put a stop to the idea, but Lady Hyleberrow changed her mind anyway.

11 Hamburg, Germany.

12 All her money had been stolen, as well as her passport. Shula asked her parents to telex money via the bank.

RECENT HISTORY

1 With what flowers did Mrs Walker replace Mrs Perkins' Easter daffodils in St Stephen's?

2 Where did Ruth, the Brookfield student, live before moving in with Mrs Antrobus?

3 Who stood against George Barford for a seat on the parish council in 1987?

4 What valuable items did Betty Tucker put in the Aldridges' dishwasher by mistake?

5 Before working for the Aldridges Mrs Walker cleaned for which member of the gentry?

6 What event, thirty years after their marriage, caused Jill to fear that Phil still thought too often of his first wife Grace Fairbrother?

7 Who was tactfully ejected from the South Borsetshire Villages Choir before *The Messiah* was staged?

8 What was the name of Helen Archer's ill-fated pony?

9 Who replaced Eddie as caller at the barn dance and kept calling his shopping list by mistake?

10 Who are the parents of Matthew Thorogood's dog?

11 What was the name of the flame-haired temptress from The Pony Club who showed more than a passing interest in Brian Aldridge?

12 Why was Bert Fry made redundant by his last employer?

A RECENT HISTORY

1   Lilies, grown by Mr Walker himself.

2   She lodged with Martha Woodford.

3   Lynda Snell. George won the seat.

4   Bone handled fish knives. Betty's surreptitious
    attempts to repair them were soon noticed.

5   Lady Lockheart. She cleaned for twenty-five years
    with never a day's complaint.

6   Phil was very anxious to meet Robin Fairbrother,
    with whom Elizabeth was in love.

7   Lynda Snell. She was fobbed off with the post of
    publicity officer.

8   Comet.

9   Nigel Pargetter.

10 He is the result of an illicit union between Captain
    (Jack Woolley's bull terrier) and Portia (Mrs
    Antrobus' Afghan).

11 Mandy Beesborough.

12 Bert's boss, a tenant farmer, was retiring and his
    land was to be taken in hand by the estate.

BROKEN HEARTS

1 Which farming boyfriend of Shula's angered Phil by telling him that Ambridge Farmers Ltd was an old-fashioned set-up?

2 When Brenda Maynard arrived in Ambridge in 1976, which marriage seemed threatened?

3 Who was seen more than once with Gemma King?

4 He was like an octopus, Shula said of this lecherous vet and former boyfriend. Who was he?

5 Shula met him on holiday and he followed her to Ambridge, disgracing her in the hunting field. What nationality was this Romeo?

6 For five years in the 1970s, Scottish Trina Muir was wined and dined by Borsetshire lads, including Brian Aldridge. What was her job?

7 Shula Archer, that Ambridge heart-breaker, shocked listeners by making love in a cornfield. With whom?

8 Who helped a policeman decorate his pine-clad kitchen, but refused to move in with him?

9 Which teenager did Lucy Perks abandon when she fell in love with Adam Macy?

10 Which visitor to Grey Gables was temptress to both Tony Archer and Detective Sergeant Barry?

11 Mary Weston broke off her engagement to which Archer?

12 Who nearly came between Tom and Pru Forrest?

A BROKEN HEARTS

1. His name was Bill Morris and he was obviously a cheeky young pup. The relationship, formed at college, didn't last long.

2. Chris and Paul Johnson's. Brenda was a former girlfriend of Paul's and appeared anxious to revive the relationship.

3. David Archer. He turned to Gemma when his relationship with Sophie Barlow went through a rocky period.

4. Martin Lambert.

5. Spanish. His name was Pedro and his English was limited.

6. She worked for Christine at the stables, where she taught Shula, among others, to ride.

7. Journalist and low-lifer Simon Parker.

8. Kathy Perks, then Kathy Holland. It took her some time to realise that she found Dave Barry totally resistable.

9. Arthur, the YTS lad at Bridge Farm.

10. Hazel Woolley.

11. Tony. She married her boss instead.

12. Bob Larkin.

1 The population of this large black and white bird has rocketed in Ambridge and elsewhere as the number of gamekeepers has declined. What is it?

2 Rabbits live in warrens, where do hares live?

3 The lapwing is often heard calling in the arable fields of Ambridge. What name, derived from its call, is the lapwing given?

4 Which conifer, grown commercially on the Bellamy Estate, loses its leaves in winter?

5 When Walter was young, all the Borsetshire children celebrated Oak-apple Day by wearing an oak-leaf. What does this day commemmorate?

6 When does the pheasant shooting season start?

7 When does the season end, and why should George have been outraged by Brian's proposal to have a shoot near to the closing date?

8 Eddie's most famous ferret was called Tex. What name is given to male ferrets?

9 Blenheim orange and Adam's pearmain are grown in Ambridge orchards. What sort of fruit are they?

10 Adam Macy was bitten by an adder. By what name is this snake otherwise known?

11 There is mistletoe in the Archers' orchard. Which tree does it grow on?

12 Where in Ambridge would you find alders?

THE COUNTRYSIDE (2)

1 The magpie is reducing the number of smaller birds in Ambridge.

2 In forms, which are nests of flattened grass. They are more solitary than rabbits.

3 Peewit, after its strange, squeaky call.

4 The larch.

5 The restoration of Charles II to the throne in 1660. He had hidden in an oak tree from pursuers after the Battle of Worcester.

6 1 October but most of the Ambridge farmers don't shoot until November.

7 The season closes on 1 February, but traditionally, to protect next season's birds, only cocks are shot after December. Hence George's anger.

8 The male is called a hob, the female a jill.

9 Apples.

10 Viper. The only poisonous British snake, it can be distinguished by the dark zigzag along its back.

11 Usually apple. It also likes poplar, oak and lime.

12 By the Am. These trees love water.

SICKNESS AND HEALTH (2)

1 How did Brian's straw-burning lead to Laura Archer wearing a surgical collar?

2 Who showed signs of addiction in The Bull – but to a fruit machine rather than to Shires?

3 Laura Archer was found frozen in a ditch with a broken ankle: she died a week later. But what was she doing in Leaders Wood in the first place?

4 Neil Carter was once rushed to hospital with Weil's disease. How did he contract it?

5 To which farmworker was Phil forced to pay compensation after he fell through the hayloft and broke his leg?

6 Who did Tom and Pru find just after he had attempted to commit suicide?

7 What illness has Walter Gabriel been afflicted by for many years?

8 Who coughs dreadfully because he suffers from an incurable agricultural disease?

9 How did Eddie's star ferret, Tex, meet his fate?

10 Who suffered considerably as he went on a sponsored diet for the church organ fund?

11 What sort of test for Down's Syndrome was carried out on Jennifer's baby: amniocentesis or chorionic villus sampling (CVS)?

12 Why was Jack Archer's job an especially unhealthy one for him?

A SICKNESS AND HEALTH (2)

1 There was a car crash because the smoke obscured Colonel Danby's vision. Laura was his passenger.

2 Tom Forrest, who wasted all his beer money on it.

3 Picking snowdrops.

4 Weil's disease can be caught from rats. In Neil's case, the infection had slipped in through a cut in his hand.

5 Jethro Larkin.

6 George Barford.

7 Diabetes.

8 Joe Grundy. He is afflicted by farmers' lung.

9 He was poisoned. George gave Eddie another ferret.

10 Tom Forrest. He raised £200 by losing half a stone.

11 Amniocenteses. CVS was still on trial and Jennifer was not selected to take part.

12 He was an alcoholic, so running a pub wasn't the best form of employment for him.

WHO IS THIS?

Can you identify the following speakers?

1 'Hello me ol' pals, me ol' beauties!'

2 'Shula dear, are you sure everything's all right?'

3 'Oh dear oh dear oh dear.'

4 'Captain. Heel. Please.'

5 'Captain. Come here you daft mutt.'

6 'Nigel. Shut up.'

7 'I won't tell a soul, m'dear.'

8 'I'm something of an expert on this.'

9 'Coo-ee!'

10 'Never mind, Lizzie. I'll open some more shampoo to cheer us up.'

11 'Wake up, dear, I've brought you some cocoa.'

12 (GRUNTS) 'What?' (STARTS) 'I wasn't asleep.'

WHO IS THIS?

1 Walter Gabriel.

2 Peggy Archer, though Jill has been known to utter these words.

3 Tom Forrest.

4 Jack Woolley.

5 Masterful George Barford.

6 Elizabeth Archer.

7 Martha Woodford.

8 Lynda Snell.

9 Jennifer Aldridge.

10 Nigel Pargetter.

11 Jill Archer.

12 Phil Archer.

Q AFFAIRS OF THE HEART

1   Who proposed to Phil Archer in 1951?

2   Which friend of his mother's did Tony jealously christen Captain Pugwash?

3   One of Neil's girlfriends planted drugs on him when police raided her party. Did he go to court?

4   Who originally objected to working with a girl, and then fell for her?

5   Between his two engagements to Shula, Mark was engaged to another. Why might this wedding have advanced his career, had it taken place?

6   Jill wrongly suspected Phil of having an affair with Myra Prestwick in 1982. How had Phil met Myra?

7   Who moved in with her boyfriend but made sure she had accommodation available to her elsewhere?

8   Elizabeth loved him but he refused to join a group holidaying in Greece when he heard she was going too. Who was this hard-hearted young man?

9   What was Robin Fairbrother's job, the next man to reject Elizabeth's affections?

10 Who advertised for a mate in a lonely hearts column and was embarrassed to receive a reply from another villager?

11 With whom did Neil suspect his fiancée Julie of philandering?

12 Which organisation did Ruth join to help her make friends and influence people?

A | AFFAIRS OF THE HEART

1   Grace Fairbrother. He felt he was too fond of farmworker Jane Maxwell at the time to accept.

2   Mr Wendover of the barn conversions, who had formerly been in the Navy.

3   Yes, and was found guilty. He was placed on probation and ordered to do community service.

4   David Archer, who fell prey to Ruth's practical charms.

5   Sarah Locke (blonde, tanned and a good skier) was the daughter of Mark's senior partner.

6   She was a fellow JP.

7   Caroline Bone, who moved to Ambridge Farm but kept a small room on at Grey Gables.

8   Tim Beauchamp.

9   He was a wine wholesaler.

10   Joe Grundy advertised himself as a gentleman farmer. Mrs Antrobus replied. Neither has breathed a word to this day.

11   Detective Sergeant Barry.

12   The local branch of the Young Farmers Club.

Q MORE WEDDINGS

1 Who was matron of honour when Martha Lily married Joby Woodford?

2 On which public holiday did this wedding take place?

3 Where was George and Christine Barford's wedding reception held?

4 When Christine married Paul Johnson in 1956, Dan discovered that part of the cost of the wedding had been borne by a third party. Who was this?

5 What was the Archer family's wedding gift to Phil and Jill?

6 In which newspaper was the announcement of Phil and Grace's wedding made in 1954?

7 Who surprised her family by opposing the marriage of George and Christine on the grounds that George was unsuitable?

8 Who told Phil she could never marry a farmer?

9 What was Brian Aldridge's wedding present to Jennifer?

10 Which bride insisted on a white wedding, although she was pregnant?

11 Who put pin-ups in Phil's suitcase as he left for his honeymoon with Jill?

12 What wedding present did Ralph Bellamy give Lilian?

A MORE WEDDINGS

1   Mrs Perkins.

2   Christmas Day.

3   Home Farm.

4   Phil. Dan was hurt and told Phil he didn't want charity from his own son.

5   A television set.

6   The *Borchester Echo*.

7   Doris Archer.

8   Jill. How wrong she was proved.

9   Twelve Jacob sheep.

10 Susan Carter.

11 His brother Jack.

12 A portrait, and a horse called Red Knight.

FARMS AND THE COUNTRYSIDE

1 Which farm did the Pounds rent and who moved in when Mary Pound left?

2 How much milk might Phil expect his cows each to yield in a year? Is it 500, 5000 or 10000 litres?

3 Mike and Betty were moving into a farmhouse as Pat and Tony were moving out. In fact, the couples were forced to share it for a few unhappy weeks. Which was the farm?

4 Brian had a Limousin, Phil a Hereford and Tony once thought of buying a Charolais. What are they?

5 Dan sold Jack and Peggy's Ambridge smallholding when they moved to Cornwall. Who was its glamorous buyer?

6 How often is the Grundys' rent reviewed?

7 Before his bankruptcy, what kind of farming did Mike Tucker specialise in?

8 Phil sends lambs to market most weeks in the summer. How old are they; three to four months, six months or a year to fifteen months?

9 The shearers move from farm to farm in Ambridge in the early summer. Who buys the fleeces?

10 Milk quotas were introduced in 1984. Phil and Tony were already producing one crop to quota. What was it?

11 Kale, mangels and maize are all eaten at times by the Grundys' cows. What sort of crops are they?

12 How many times a day does Tony milk his cows?

A FARMS AND THE COUNTRYSIDE

1 Ambridge Farm. The Tuckers rented it from the Bellamy Estate after the Pounds.

2 5000 litres a year is about the national average.

3 Willow Farm.

4 Not cars but breeds of beef-cattle, and specifically here, bulls.

5 Carol Grey. Scandalously, she drove a sports car.

6 Every three years. This is true of all the tenant farmers in England and Wales.

7 He was a dairy farmer.

8 Three to four months.

9 The British Wool Marketing Board.

10 Potatoes. Each year the Potato Marketing Board tells Phil and Tony how many acres they may grow.

11 Forage crops, as they are grown to be grazed or fed to stock.

12 Twice, like all the other farmers in Ambridge. Some people milk three times a day.

Q CLOSE SHAVES

1 Who, in an act of uncharacteristic foolishness, ate three death cap toadstools, thinking they were mushrooms?

2 Who was reluctantly leaving Ambridge when he was attacked by gypsies and had to rest at The Bull?

3 Who had to leave Ambridge because he owed Jack Woolley so much money?

4 Who had an out-of-body experience while Mrs Snell was administering the kiss of life?

5 Who in 1958 was missing, presumed dead, after reports that her boat had capsized off the Danish coast during a sailing holiday?

6 Which disease kept Peggy Archer in Felpersham Isolation Hospital one Christmas?

7 What catastrophe forced Shula's coming of age party to be cancelled?

8 Eddie, unusually, was paid to work at Brookfield when both Phil and Jethro were ill in 1982. What was wrong with them?

9 Who fell off his kitchen roof and concussed himself?

10 Who was suspected by the village bobby of vandalising a phone box and spray-painting a signpost?

11 Why did Eddie Grundy get into big trouble as treasurer of the country'n'western club?

12 Name the only villager ever wanted by Interpol.

CLOSE SHAVES

1   Colonel Danby. He had to have his stomach pumped.

2   John Tregorran.

3   Nelson. He left because he didn't want Walter to find out. When Walter did find out, Nelson returned to repay his debts.

4   Jack Woolley. He was later fitted with a pacemaker.

5   Carol Grey.

6   Diphtheria.

7   Jill had been rushed to hospital, critically ill with myxoedema and an acute kidney infection.

8   A battery had exploded. As a result Phil had to have an operation on his right eye and Jethro suffered from shock and cuts.

9   Jack Woolley. Some say he hasn't been the same since.

10 Neil Carter. His cupboards at Brookfield were searched without his permission and in spite of strong objections from Jill.

11 He raided the funds for beer money.

12 Nelson Gabriel, of course.

Q MORE QUESTIONS FROM THE 1980s

1   Whose girlfriend demonstrated against his methods of farming?

2   Why did Jack and Caroline have to feed organic farmers on non-organic produce?

3   Why did Elizabeth have to postpone her nineteenth birthday party, to her disgust?

4   What parts did Danby and Tom play in Pat's feminist *Cinderella* (a production which never reached the stage)?

5   Susan Carter hasn't yet taken her driving test, but how many times has Clarrie Grundy done so?

6   What piece of machinery has enabled David to start his own contracting business?

7   What is the name given by Elizabeth to the boss of the *Borchester Echo* Tele-ad Sales Department?

8   Which song can Tom Forrest be relied upon to sing, if urged strongly, at the Christmas revue and the Harvest Supper?

9   Who were the organisers of the 1988 village fête?

10 Where did Neil and Susan Carter live when they were first married?

11 What was Eddie searching for when he raided Woodbine Cottage shortly after Jethro's death?

12 Who sleeps in black satin sheets?

A MORE QUESTIONS FROM THE 1980s

1 Neil's girlfriend Vicki was a member of the Borchester Animal Defence Protest Group, and she strongly objected to his keeping battery hens.

2 The choosy Jean-Paul insisted on serving vegetables (like mangetouts) which were almost impossible to obtain organically grown.

3 Her grandfather had just died.

4 The ugly sisters.

5 Once. She passed first time.

6 His digger.

7 Morgan the Gorgon.

8 'The Village Pump'. He has a wide repertoire but this is the villagers' favourite.

9 Kathy Perks and Lynda Snell.

10 Nightingale Farm.

11 Jethro's coin collection (subsequently proved worthless). He was also interested in any Post Office books he might find.

12 Nelson Gabriel – when he's at his Borchester flat. He doesn't bring them to Honeysuckle Cottage with him.

Q MARRIAGES

1　What was Martha's surname before she married Joby Woodford?

2　John and Carol Tregorran eventually married fifteen years after he first proposed to her. During that fifteen years, whom had each married?

3　Who married for the second time three years before his daughter married for the first time?

4　Jennifer was not married when she was pregnant with Adam. When did she marry his father?

5　Both Mrs P's husbands have been called Perkins by a strange twist of fate. How did she meet Arthur, her second husband?

6　Did Lucy Perks agree to go to her father's wedding?

7　Which Archer was mourning her husband's death less than a year after she married him?

8　Who forgot his first wedding anniversary?

9　Why was a policeman's wedding reception held at Home Farm?

10　What present did the young Archers give Phil and Jill for their silver wedding anniversary?

11　According to Phil Archer a girl called Marianne Peters seemed to be seeing too much of a married man. Which married man?

12　Which couple didn't marry, but lived together at The Lodge?

A MARRIAGES

1. Lily. Her first husband was a postman at Penny Hassett.

2. John married district nurse Janet Sheldon, Carol married landowner Charles Grenville.

3. George Fairbrother, father of Grace, married Helen Carey in 1952. Grace at first disapproved of the match.

4. Trick question, she never did. Adam's father was Paddy Redmond, an itinerant farmworker, but Adam later took the name of Jennifer's first husband, Travers-Macy.

5. He'd come to Ambridge to work on Grace Fairbrother's memorial window in the village church.

6. Yes, although it took a great deal of persuasion.

7. Lilian. She married Canadian pilot Lester Nicholson in 1969. He died falling downstairs in hospital where he was receiving treatment for his deteriorating eyesight.

8. Mark Hebden.

9. PC Coverdale was marrying Eva Lenz, au pair to the Aldridges.

10. A silver candelabrum.

11. Paul Johnson, Christine's husband.

12. George Barford and Nora Salt.

Q

AMBRIDGE GARDENS (2)

1   Why did Walter tell Nelson to pick off and discard his unopened blackcurrant buds?

2   Elizabeth Archer insists that impatiens was named after her. By what name is it otherwise known?

3   Jill wanted the gardening club to visit Vita Sackville-West's garden. Where is it?

4   Clarrie would like to grow a garden in a bottle. Mrs Snell informed her of the correct name for this. What is it?

5   Mrs Perkins grows daffodils, and Mrs Snell grows narcissi. What is the difference?

6   Moles are always popping up to ruin the rolling lawns at Grey Gables. What do they eat?

7   Peggy Archer bought herself some golden queen holly expecting it to have berries. Why didn't it?

8   Phil's favourite eating-apple has a distinctive rough skin. What is it called?

9   The decline of Borsetshire coppicing means that traditional pea and bean sticks are no longer available to local gardeners. Which wood did they once use for these sticks?

10 Which tree produces conkers and attracts groups of little boys who try to knock them down?

11 What is deadheading?

12 Which blooms perfume the garden at Brookfield after dark?

A AMBRIDGE GARDENS (2)

1 The bushes were suffering from big bud, a disease spread by the tiny gall mite.

2 Busy lizzie.

3 Sissinghurst Castle, in Kent.

4 A terrarium.

5 No difference. Mrs Snell just thinks daffodil sounds common.

6 Worms.

7 Golden queen is mis-named: it's a male holly, golden king is the female and therefore has the berries.

8 Russet.

9 Hazel.

10 Horse chestnut.

11 Taking off the faded blooms to encourage the plants to flower more.

12 Night scented stock, primarily. Also honeysuckle, evening primrose and tobacco plants.

Q GENERAL QUESTIONS (6)

1 A sweepstake was held in The Bull in 1987. What was it in aid of?

2 Glamorous Jane Maxwell, who helped Phil on the Bellamy Estate, lodged with which villager?

3 Who owned the village stores and Post Office before Jack Woolley?

4 On what flimsy evidence was it once claimed that Shakespeare visited Ambridge?

5 Name the cottage which Sid and Polly Perks bought at Penny Hassett as an investment.

6 In 1967, what educational cause did Jill espouse?

7 What did Jackie Smith, Nora McAuley and Clarrie Larkin all have in common?

8 What did country'n'western heart-throb Jolene Rogers call her baby girl?

9 When Shula became agent to the Bellamy Estate, she replaced Andrew Sinclair . . . but who was farm manager at the time?

10 Who decided not to learn to drive a car in the mid-1960s, and drove a pony and trap instead?

11 There have been various appeals for repairs to St Stephen's over the years. In 1974 what was the appeal for?

12 What sort of oven does Jill have?

A

GENERAL QUESTIONS (6)

1 To pay for the vicar's disasterous attempt to print postcards of the church. There was a printing error and the cards could not be sold or their cost reclaimed.

2 Mrs Perkins, who found her too posh by half, not least because Jane didn't help with the washing-up.

3 Sid and Polly Perks.

4 While redecorating at The Bull, Sid allegedly found two pages of *Hollinshed's Chronicles* (1587), with scribbles in the margin referring to a George Bardolfe.

5 Rose Cottage.

6 She took an active part in the campaign to stop Borchester Grammar going independent.

7 They were all barmaids at The Bull. Clarrie still works there.

8 Fallon.

9 Bobby Waters. He retired soon afterwards.

10 Doris Archer.

11 Repairs to the roof and rehanging of the bells. Ralph Bellamy donated a substantial amount.

12 An Aga.

HARD QUESTIONS

1 What was Pru Forrest's maiden name?

2 Peggy Archer lay in hospital in 1953: with whom was her husband Jack supposed to be having an affair?

3 Two villagers have called their dogs Gyp. One was Jethro Larkin. Who was the other?

4 Who originally formed Ambridge Farmers Ltd?

5 Jennifer Archer returned from Cornwall and caused upset at the village school. Why?

6 Name the part-time typist who works at the Bellamy Estate office.

7 The Archer family went to a point-to-point in 1958 to watch Paul Johnson riding Monarch. Mysteriously, Doris didn't turn up. Why not?

8 Name the two well-known cart-horses who pulled Letty Lawson-Hope to her funeral in 1958.

9 Which London estate agency sold Ambridge Hall to the Snells for Laura Archer's heir?

10 Pru Forrest has not been heard on the air for many years . . . except for a few brief words to mark which event?

11 Can you name the ventriloquist's dummy that Doris gave to Walter as a birthday present in 1965?

12 Jill Archer drove into a pedestrian in 1977. It was not her fault and no one was hurt, so why was she reluctant to confess to Phil?

A HARD QUESTIONS

1 Harris.

2 Elsie Catcher, a teacher at the village school who had been helping with the children while Peggy was away.

3 Zebedee Tring, the old roadman.

4 Dan, Fred Barrett and Jess Allard. Jess soon died, and the set-up was then Dan, Phil and Fred.

5 She was wearing her private school blazer and hat.

6 Mrs Short. She is supervised by Peggy Archer.

7 She had gone to have her teeth out without telling Dan.

8 Boxer and Blossom.

9 Ling and Adair.

10 Her sweeping victory at the flower and produce show in 1982. Her victory was so sweeping that she was suspected of cheating.

11 Marmaduke. Whatever became of him?

12 Her driving licence was out of date. She need not have worried, no action was taken.

Q BEHIND THE SCENES

1   Who created *The Archers*?

2   Scriptwriter Bruno Milna is much better-known by another name. Who is he?

3   Who was producer of the programme for twenty-eight years?

4   The dramatic death of Grace in 1955 stole the limelight from which landmark in broadcasting history?

5   Which thrilling serial did *The Archers* replace?

6   When was the first episode broadcast?

7   Although it was subsequently called Brookfield Farm, the Archer heartland had a different name during the programme's trial run. What was it?

8   On which channel was *The Archers* first heard. Was it Home, Light or Third?

9   For more than ten years *The Archers* was scripted by two writers. Who were they?

10 Which serial was, for many years, *The Archers'* rival radio soap?

11 When was the programme's first agricultural editor appointed?

12 Where is *The Archers* recorded?

BEHIND THE SCENES

1 Godfrey Baseley.

2 Norman Painting, who plays Phil Archer.

3 Tony Shryane.

4 The launch of ITV. The programme's editor insisted that this was pure coincidence.

5 *Dick Barton.*

6 Six trial episodes were made in Whit week, 1950. Daily broadcasts began on 1 January, 1951.

7 Wimberton Farm.

8 Light. The Sunday omnibus edition moved to the Home Service in the early 1960s.

9 Geoffrey Webb and Edward J Mason.

10 *Mrs Dale's Diary.*

11 1972. It was and still is Anthony Parkin. Until that date the programme's editor, Godfrey Baseley, had overseen agricultural content.

12 Pebble Mill in Birmingham.

Q THE ACTORS

1 Name the actors who have played Dan Archer?

2 Before daily broadcasts of *The Archers* began, the BBC produced six trial episodes of the programme. Which of the actors who took part in these episodes is still in the programme today?

3 Who played Phil's ill-fated first wife, Grace? What part in *The Archers* did the same actress play later?

4 Farmer and TV personality Ted Moult auditioned for the part of Dan Archer. But which part was created for him instead?

5 Which well-known countrywoman plays Martha?

6 Lesley Saweard took over the part of Christine in 1953: her voice exactly matched that of the previous actress. Who was this?

7 Heather Bell and Fiona Mathieson played Clarrie Grundy. Can you name the third actress to take the part, and the other radio soap opera in which she starred?

8 The *Archers* actors are in which union?

9 Charles Collingwood, who plays Brian Aldridge is married to which other member of the cast?

10 Who are the real life father and daughter who play a father and daughter in *The Archers*?

11 Who has Chriss Gittins played since 1953?

12 Hedli Niklaus played Libby Jones the milk recorder, then Eva the au pair before landing her current part. Which character does she play?

THE ACTORS

1   Harry Oakes, Monte Crick, Edgar Harrison and Frank Middlemass.

2   Norman Painting who plays Phil, and June Spencer who plays Peggy.

3   Ysanne Churchman. She later played Mary Pound, tenant of Ambridge Farm, among other smaller parts.

4   Bill Insley, retired Derbyshire farmer and tempter of Martha Woodford.

5   Mollie Harris.

6   Pamela Mant.

7   Rosalind Adams, who played Tracy in the now defunct Radio 2 soap, *Waggoners' Walk*.

8   Equity.

9   Judy Bennett, who plays Shula.

10 Alan Devereux and his daughter Tracy-Jane White play publican Sid and his daughter Lucy.

11 Walter Gabriel.

12 Kathy Perks.

MORE QUESTIONS FROM BEHIND THE SCENES

1 In 1983, a character from another soap opera appeared in Ambridge. Which soap?

2 Who took Mark and Shula's wedding pictures?

3 Which Sunday evening television programme was broadcast from Ambridge in 1988?

4 How many episodes does each writer script at a time?

5 How much of *The Archers* is recorded on location?

6 How much is cut from the daily episodes of *The Archers* to make the Sunday omnibus?

7 What is the name of *The Archers* signature tune?

8 A real pub is frequently used as The Bull for photographic purposes. It is called The Old Bull. Where is it?

9 In the 1980s, where was a successful theatrical version of *The Archers* staged?

10 In 1987 two child actors joined the cast. What parts do they play?

11 Spot effects are used in the making of *The Archers*. What are they?

12 Is *The Archers* broadcast in mono or in stereo?

A MORE QUESTIONS FROM BEHIND THE SCENES

1   Jenny Stewart from the Radio Scotland serial, *Kilbreck*. Nelson fell for her and Caroline later visited her during the Edinburgh Festival.

2   Patrick Lichfield.

3   *Songs of Praise*.

4   Five. Each writer is responsible for one week's broadcasts.

5   Almost none of it. Only very special occasions justify the expense.

6   A total of 15 minutes is cut from the 75 minutes broadcast on weekdays.

7   'Barwick Green'.

8   The village of Inkberrow. (However, Ambridge is not based on Inkberrow.)

9   The Watermill Theatre, Newbury. When the show transferred to a big top in Battersea, it was not so successful.

10 John and Helen Archer. The actors are Sam Barriscale and Frances Graham.

11 The sound effects made in the studio by human hand, like the clinking of crockery. Other effects, like sheep bleating, are on disc.

12 It is the only radio drama still broadcast in mono. Stereo takes much longer to record.